DEVON WHITE

GARY SHEFFIELD

CRAIG COUNSELL

EDGAR RENTERIA

DARREN DAULTON

MOISES ALOU

AL LEITER

WORLD SERIES CHAMPIONS
MIAMI MARLINS

BOBBY BONILLA

CHARLES JOHNSON

WORLD SERIES GAME 7 PLAYED ON SUNDAY,
OCTOBER 26, 1997, AT PRO PLAYER STADIUM. THE
MARLINS DEFEATED THE INDIANS BY A SCORE OF
3–2 TO WIN THE WORLD CHAMPIONSHIP.

WORLD SERIES CHAMPIONS

MIAMI MARLINS

SARA GILBERT

CREATIVE EDUCATION

Published by Creative Education
P.O. Box 227, Mankato, Minnesota 56002
Creative Education is an imprint of The Creative Company
www.thecreativecompany.us

Design and production by Blue Design (www.bluedes.com)
Art direction by Rita Marshall
Printed in the United States of America

Photographs by Getty Images (Joel Auerbach, Al Bello, Lisa
Blumenfeld, Angelo Cavalli, Tom DiPace/Sports Illustrated,
Stephen Dunn, Elsa, Steve Green/MLB Photos, Drew Hallowell,
Jeff Haynes/AFP, Jed Jacobsohn, Nick Laham, Mitchell Layton,
Mitchell Layton/MLB Photos, Ronald C. Modra/Sports Imagery,
Doug Pensinger, Rich Pilling/MLB Photos, Eliot J. Schechter, Ezra
Shaw, Don Smith/MLB Photos, Jamie Squire, Matthew Stockman,
Rhona Wise/AFP, Mike Zarrilli)

Library of Congress Cataloging-in-Publication Data
Gilbert, Sara.
Miami Marlins / Sara Gilbert.
p. cm. — (World series championships)
Includes bibliographical references and index.
Summary: A simple introduction to the Miami Marlins major
league baseball team, including its start in 1993, its World Series
triumphs, and its stars throughout the years.
ISBN 978-1-60818-264-0
1. Florida Marlins (Baseball team)—History—Juvenile literature. I.
Title.
GV875.F6G55 2012
796.357'6409759381—dc23   2012001753

First edition
9 8 7 6 5 4 3 2 1

Cover: Shortstop Hanley Ramirez
Page 2: First baseman Gaby Sanchez
Page 3: Shortstop Edgar Renteria
Right: The Marlins' old park, Joe Robbie Stadium

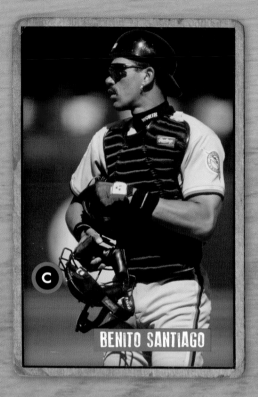

C

BENITO SANTIAGO

CF

CHRIS COGHLAN

P

KEVIN BROWN

LF

CLIFF FLOYD

2B

DAN UGGLA

CF

PRESTON WILSON

TABLE OF CONTENTS

MIAMI AND MARLINS PARK

Miami is a city next to the Atlantic Ocean in Florida. It is a popular vacation spot. Marlins Park is also a popular place to visit. It is the home field for a baseball team called the Marlins.

RIVALS AND COLORS

The Marlins play major league baseball. Thirty major-league teams try to become world champions by winning the World Series. The Marlins' uniforms used to be black, TEAL, silver, and white. Now they are black, white, orange, yellow, and blue. The Marlins' biggest RIVALS are the Atlanta Braves.

2003 WORLD SERIES

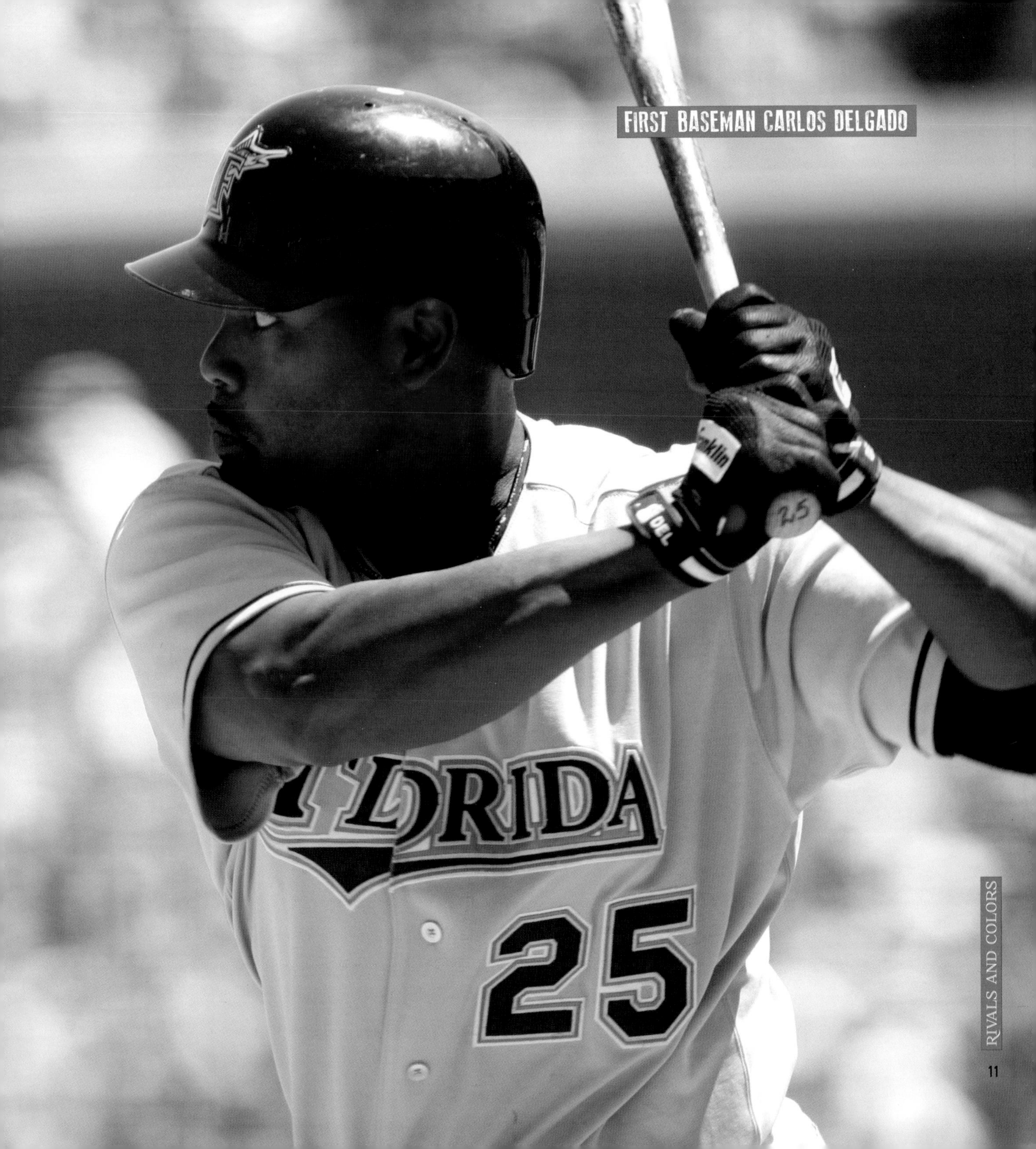

FIRST BASEMAN CARLOS DELGADO

MARLINS HISTORY

The Marlins joined the National League in 1993. Exciting players like catcher Benito Santiago were fun to watch. But the Marlins lost more games than they won for the first few years.

CATCHER CHARLES JOHNSON

JACK McKEON

JOSH BECKETT

ALEX GONZALEZ

A. J. BURNETT

MIKE LOWELL

BOBBY BONILLA

In 1997, new manager Jim Leyland led the Marlins to the
PLAYOFFS. They surprised everyone when they beat two teams.
Then they won the World Series by beating the Cleveland
Indians, too!

DONTRELLE WILLIS

The Marlins dropped to last place the next year. They were a bad team for a few seasons. But in 2003, the Marlins were back! Pitcher Dontrelle Willis helped the UNDERDOG Marlins beat the New York Yankees in the World Series.

Second baseman Dan Uggla hit a lot of home runs to make the Marlins a tough team for the next several years. But they could not get back to the playoffs or the World Series.

DAN UGGLA

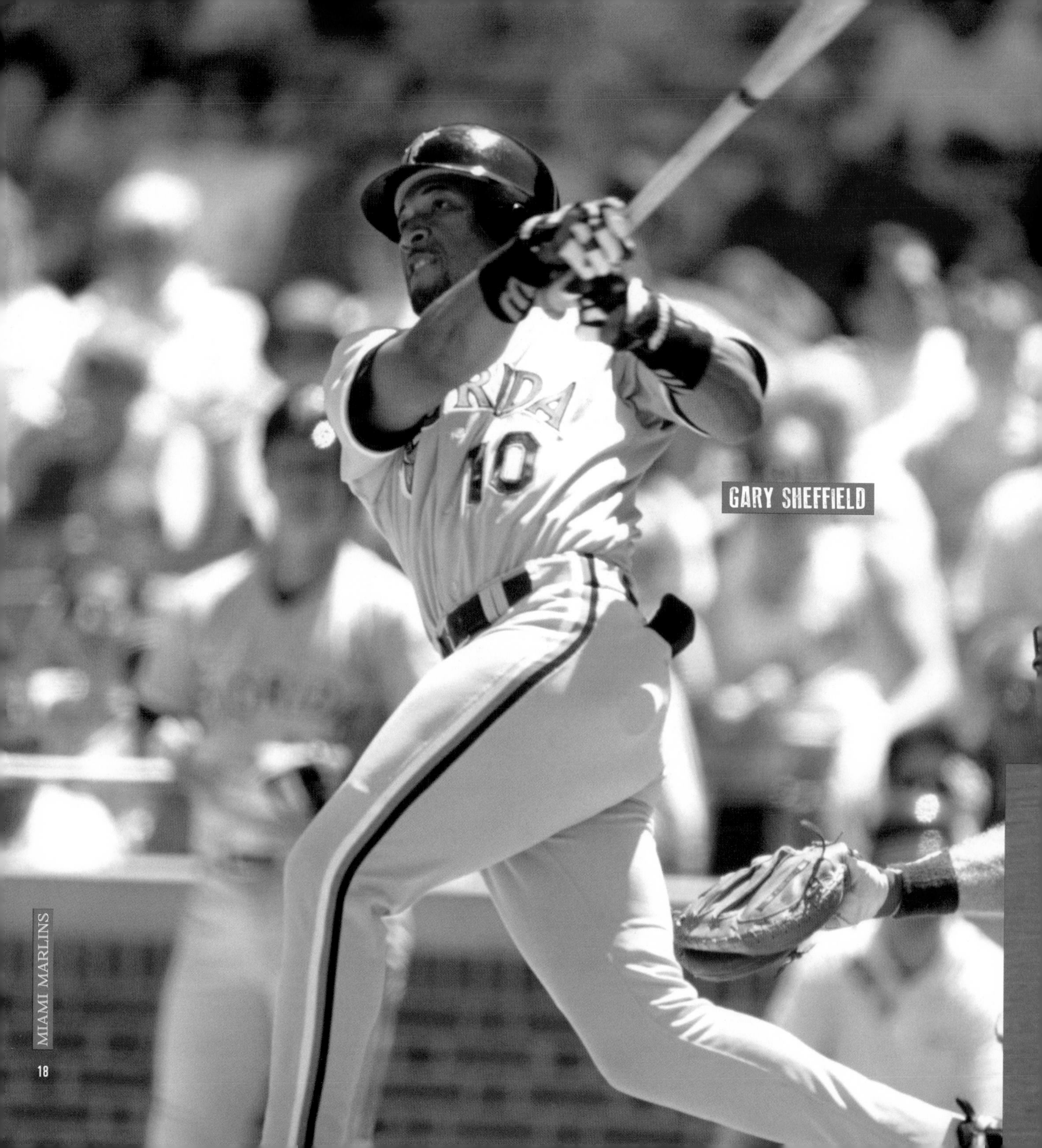

GARY SHEFFIELD

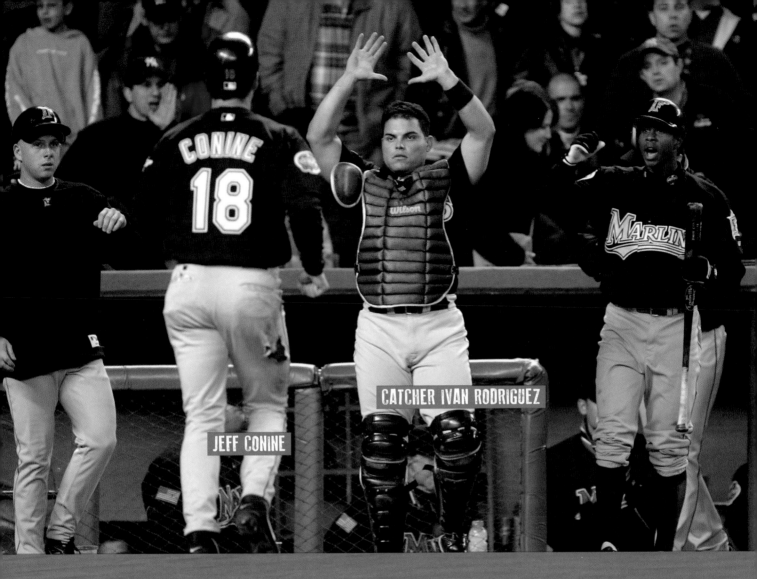

JEFF CONINE

CATCHER IVAN RODRIGUEZ

MARLINS STARS

Big outfielder Jeff Conine played in all 162 games during the
Marlins' first season. Fans in Florida called him "Mr. Marlin." Fans
loved watching outfielder Gary Sheffield slam home runs, too. He
hit 122 homers for the Marlins.

In 1996, second baseman Luis Castillo joined the Marlins. His speed and HUSTLE on the field made him a star. He played with first baseman Derrek Lee. Lee was tall and could hit the ball hard.

Powerful outfielder Giancarlo Stanton joined the Marlins in 2010. In 2012, he blasted a home run that went almost 500 feet! Fans hoped that he could lead Miami to another World Series!

DERREK LEE

GIANCARLO STANTON

PITCHER JOSH JOHNSON

HOW THE MARLINS GOT THEIR NAME

The Marlins are named after a long fish with a pointed, spearlike nose. Marlins are found in the ocean near Miami. The team used to be called the Florida Marlins. Now it is called the Miami Marlins. Many Miami fans simply call the Marlins "The Fish."

ABOUT THE MARLINS

First season: 1993

League/division: National League, East Division

World Series championships:

1997	*4 games to 3 versus Cleveland Indians*
2003	*4 games to 2 versus New York Yankees*

Marlins Web site for kids:

http://mlb.mlb.com/mlb/kids/index.jsp?c_id=fla

Club MLB:

http://web.clubmlb.com/index.html

GLOSSARY

HUSTLE — moving fast or trying hard to get a job done

PLAYOFFS — all the games (including the World Series) after the regular season that are played to decide who the champion will be

RIVALS — teams that play extra hard against each other

TEAL — a dark, greenish-blue color

UNDERDOG — a person or team that is not expected to win

INDEX